NAPOLEON

BONAPARTE

A Fascinating Biography

SIMON JOHNSON

TABLE OF CONTENTS

INTRODUCTION

<hr>

Napoleon Bonaparte, also known as Napoleon I, is considered to be one of the greatest military leaders in history. He is also among the most celebrated persons throughout the history of the West. His gradual rise to fame through his contribution in various wars makes for spectacular records in history, and his story is one that continues being told one generation after another.

Napoleon is undoubtedly not one of the regular war veterans. His tact and skills made him among the best military geniuses that ever existed, enabling him to win several wars and attain the status of emperor. His journey to the top of the military ladder began when he enrolled in military school, with some of the unfortunate occurrences, such as bullying, propelling him to gain courage and strive to always defeat anyone who was against him.

Napoleon is known for his contribution to the European army through the providing of modern and professional conscript armies. Unlike many leaders who are selfish and self-centered, Napoleon's ideology was always inclined to ensuring that the needs of the people were always put first. As you will find out from this read, Napoleon had many challenges, particularly when it came to the wars and the many people in authority who attempted to silence him since they were afraid of his skills. However, it was his determination and constant drive to excel in the face of adversities that made him one of the greatest warriors that ever lived, and the world knows his name. From a poor simple military boy, Napoleon grew to become one of the most notable emperors that France ever had. This biography will provide a detailed analysis into the life of Napoleon— from his personal life to the many wars that he fought and won, and the decision-making process that guaranteed him constant victory.

CHAPTER 1

EARLY AND PERSONAL LIFE

<figure>◆◆◆</figure>

Early Life

Napoleon Bonaparte (August 15, 1769–May 5, 1821) was the second surviving son of Carlo Bonaparte and Letizia Ramolino, born on the island of Corsica (Thompson, 2018). His father was a well-renowned lawyer, and the family was relatively well-off. In addition to his law career, Carlo also served in the French administration. The Bonaparte lineage was considered to be noble, and the family was counted as being among the few elites in the port city. Despite their status, the family lived frugally, and Napoleon admitted that at one point, he felt very disappointed with his parents. Their quest for a simple and gentle life was too much, and Napoleon felt that they could have afforded to provide him and his siblings a much better life. Living together crammed in a few rooms that were in a very old house was not really what most noble families would choose. Much later, Napoleon would admit that he eventually became accustomed to the lifestyle and that he even grew a little too fond of it than he anticipated.

Where Carlo Bonaparte lacked in terms of giving his children a robust and affluent livelihood, he compensated with pushing his sons and encouraging them to aim for greater heights. Napoleon did not need much pushing, as he was very focused and determined to prosper on his own accord. The passion lived on despite the many challenges that he faced, one of them being the constant bullying that he faced when he enrolled in a military academy at the age of nine.

The military school was based in France, which automatically made Napoleon an outsider among all the other students. Also, social barriers became evident. During his time, most people who enrolled in military academies were from affluent and noble families, of which Napoleon was a part of. However, unlike him, the other participants came from families who lived in a manner that highlighted their nobility and high social status. Since Napoleon's family lived frugally, the schoolmates dubbed him dubious and constantly taunted him. Also, the fact that Napoleon grew up speaking Italian gave him an accent that came out with his poor French, further making him a subject of ridicule.

Napoleon's experiences in the military school, although terrible for a young boy, ultimately came to serve as one of the factors that largely shaped his character, as shall be seen throughout this book. First, the fact that he was a loner made him stronger on his own and devoid of relying on anyone for anything. Also, Napoleon developed a very defensive arrogance, which was evident in his interactions in the course of his duties. Most importantly, since he was always subject to ridicule and had to defend himself, Napoleon continually developed tactics that aimed at outsmarting the bullies. The tendency continued, and throughout his fights, Napoleon was always very open to the ideas that could help him outsmart his enemies. In 1785, Napoleon graduated. In the same year, while still in France, his father passed on, and Napoleon had to assume the role of head of the family, a factor that resulted in imminent financial hardship. Still, Napoleon was stronger than ever. The military positions that followed established his career as one of the most prolific military experts in history, and soon Napoleon Bonaparte was a household name.

Personal Life

Marriage to Josephine

Napoleon Bonaparte might have been an expert when it came to war, but that did not mean that he had no heart for love. In 1795, he met a widow who had just lost her husband and was the mistress of one of the most powerful men in France. The man, Paul Barras, was seemingly unresponsive to her love, and when Napoleon expressed interest, he encouraged it. Josephine, the mistress, gradually responded to Napoleon's pursuits, although it was just for convenience. Since Barras had discarded her, she just wanted security as well as financial support for herself and the children. Napoleon, on the other hand, deeply loved the woman and showed her compassion and empathy. He was delighted to be with her and did not care that she potentially did not love him as much. Napoleon was a hopeless romantic who illustrated signs of constant fantasies. In one famous romantic letter addressed to Josephine, Napoleon asserted how he always awoke full of her and how the memories of the pleasures they shared left eternal rest to his senses. In 1796, Napoleon proposed to her, and they were married on March 9.

Napoleon's affection toward Josephine was not only unrequited but was also immensely eventful. While Napoleon wrote many letters when he was away on official duty, Josephine rarely wrote back. Further, the lady began an affair with another man the same year that she got married, and Napoleon eventually got wind of what was happening. It is said that his feelings changed in entirety soon after realizing what she was doing, and the burning flame that was once there was wholly extinguished.

It took two years for Napoleon to come to terms with the fact that his wife had cheated on him. As revenge, Napoleon began an affair with a beautiful married woman in 1798, the woman popularly known as Cleopatra. Cleopatra showed Napoleon a deep and intimate kind of love to a level that Josephine had never even been close enough to experience. As a result, Napoleon's marriage to Josephine dwindled even more, and he stopped sending love letters or even attempting to show Josephine any kind of love. Notably, Cleopatra wasn't his only mistress, although she was the first woman that Napoleon had developed an affair with after his failed marriage. Soon after, Napoleon is known to have had even more sexual relationships with several other women.

Despite the rampant infidelity and problems in his marriage, Napoleon proved to be a man of class and stature when he remained true to his role as a husband. Without a doubt, there is a very high possibility that he would have been faithful had Josephine not been unfaithful to him in the first place. So seemingly committed and true was he that when he was elected emperor in 1804, he allowed his unfaithful wife to be crowned empress.

Though committed, the relationship never healed, and Napoleon continued being unfaithful right until the time when the two divorced in 1809. The basis of the divorce was not infidelity, but rather that Josephine had failed to conceive a child, and Napoleon was in dire need of an heir. Surprisingly, the divorce was entirely amicable, and Napoleon even allowed Josephine to retain the title of empress for good. In his words, Napoleon wished for Josephine never to doubt all the sentiments that he had given her earlier on when they were happy. Also, it was his wish that, even with the divorce, Josephine would hold him as her best and dearest friend.

Marriage to Marie Louise

Marie Louise was the second wife of Napoleon Bonaparte who reigned as the empress of the French beginning in 1810. The main reason as to why Napoleon chose to marry her was not out of deep love, as it had been in his first marriage, but rather as an attempt to sire an heir. Initially, Marie was not even his first choice, and he had only decided to marry her when he got tired of the delay in marriage approval from one of the leading royal families in Europe. At the time of the marriage, Marie Louise didn't know who Napoleon was in-depth, and the only reason she married him was so she could fulfill the wishes of her family and elders. The wedding brought very favorable inferences as France and Austria ended up developing solid ties.

Marie and Napoleon got married in an Augustinian church in 1810, and their wedding was not only full of color but also involved some of the most affluent people in the community. The wedding party was so magnificent that it ranked among the most brilliant festivities that had ever been conducted in the community. Marie was only a teenager, but she handled her affairs so well that Napoleon began admiring her. While their marriage was not based on love from the onset, their romantic relationship soon began to grow, although it was not half as profound as the affection that Napoleon had shown to his first wife. Also, there was no infidelity, as Marie remained faithful to her vows. However, the marriage was not without its own set of issues, as Napoleon consistently regarded Marie as being too shy in comparison with his first wife—sentiments that hurt her. Also, the fact that he was still in constant communication with Josephine always upset Marie, threatening the marriage.

In July 1810, Marie realized that she was pregnant, much to the delight of many people, and most especially Napoleon. In 1811, a boy was born and he was named Napoleon Francoise Bonaparte. Since he was royal, he was automatically given the title of the King of Rome. The birth had been very sensitive and difficult, and Napoleon felt that he was not ready to have other children if Marie would suffer so much. The fact that she had given him a son made him soften more towards her. The two remained married up until his death.

CHAPTER 2

MILITARY CAREER

◆◈◈◆

Initial Role as a Second Lieutenant

As soon as Napoleon graduated from military school, he went on to become a second lieutenant in the artillery regiment. For some reason, Napoleon was not quite assiduous in the service as a second lieutenant, and at the end of his service, he had accumulated thirty-eight months of absence in comparison to just thirty-three months when he was present.

During the period when Napoleon was serving as second lieutenant, there was an outbreak of a revolution that saw the end of military occupation of Corsica, a military operation that had begun in 1769. Notably, Napoleon was an avid Corsican nationalist, and he vowed to fight for his country of origin (de Bourrienne, 2012). During the early stages of the revolution, Napoleon spent his time fighting a complex struggle that was among the royalists, revolutionists, and the Corsican nationalists. Between the three groups, the Corsican nationalists have the least number of fighters because the nationals were not only more disadvantaged than the rest but also because most of the qualified army officials were fighting for the other groups. Despite the shortcomings, the biggest advantage was that there were plenty of volunteers who were ready to fight for Corsica, and all they needed was a leader. Napoleon took on the role of commander and was intent on helping the volunteers win the war.

One of the reasons Napoleon was so against the French invasion of Corsica was the administration and absolutism that was bestowed upon the Corsican as well as the disregard to their preferred way of life. Before the invasion, Corsica had been an independent nation and had its system of governance. Since Napoleon had grown up in the country, he was greatly fascinated by its history and the stories he read about how his country used to operate before the invasion. Napoleon was very passionate about restoring the lost glory of his country, hence the determination to fight the war. Ultimately, not only was Napoleon successful in helping win the war, but he also gained wide accolades and status among the military officials. By the end of the war, Napoleon had already been promoted to commander in the French army.

Rise to Power

It was while Napoleon was a commander in the French army that he proved his skill and expertise. In 1792, there was an increased revolution between France and various nations in Europe. The military conflicts and tension had always been in existence, but it is only in 1792 that the war became mainstream and absolute. Napoleon made preparations with the army under his command, and in 1796, he made advances that began the war. During this time, the major rival was the Austrian army, and Napoleon was able to defeat it quite easily. The war had not been easy, and Napoleon had to face the opponents in a series of battles, particularly in Italy. By 1797, Austria had conceded defeat, and the result was a signed treaty with the French that resulted in territorial gains and a win for the French. This battle was very revolutionary, and it marked the stepping stone in recognition of Napoleon as an exceptional commander.

So exceptional was Napoleon's commandeering that he was approached by some of the senior-most commanders in France to lead an invasion in England. The senior commanders comprised of a group of five top-notch individuals that had governed France for several years. This directory was very oblivious of the risks a sudden invasion held, and Napoleon was able to change their minds by explaining how the sudden invasion would work against them. At the time, the French army had just won a battle against Austria, and it was not strong enough to fight another battle just yet. Also, there was not enough workforce for such an extensive war, and Napoleon knew that if they invaded England at the time, they would be highly outnumbered and defeated. Such trivial information turned out to be quite beneficial for the overall French army, and Napoleon was able to study war plans extensively and come up with a better strategy that guaranteed the French army even more success. In this case, the best strategy was to conquer Egypt first and wipe the British trade routes to weaken the European forces. The directory was impressed with the analysis and decision-making skills showcased by Napoleon, and they agreed to follow his strategy.

Napoleon in Egypt

Napoleon's expedition to Egypt was aimed solely at achieving two critical things. The first was to re-establish the expected wars that had been put on a temporary pause between the French revolutionary army and the European forces. At that time, Napoleon had already foreshadowed an imminent defeat where they had to advance towards the European army, seeing that they neither had the workforce nor resources required to fight a winning battle. The second critical thing was to secure their position by blocking Britain's trade route to India, which would leave them devoid of the necessary resources that they required to finance a war.

Notably, one of the reasons why Napoleon was so hard-pressed to fight the battle in Egypt successfully was that it had always been his dream to lead a war in the Middle East and come out of it victorious. The battle through Egypt provided the perfect opportunity, and Napoleon was determined to prove that he could win any war that he set his mind to. Not only would the conquest in Egypt enable the French to get a hold over the Mediterranean, but it would also serve as the perfect route to attack Britain when they were least aware of what was happening.

Notably, the directory was not as happy about Napoleon's vigor and courage as one would have thought. Since Napoleon was a great army commander and had amassed the support and admiration of thousands where he was known, these leaders knew that he posed a very serious threat and that eventually he could oust them easily and take up the leadership position. While these leaders wanted victory over the British, their selfish interests took precedence, as they valued their positions in government more than retaining a skilled war leader such as Napoleon. Therefore, when they sent him out to the war, they were sure that it would keep him busy for a while, making their positions more secure. Further, there was always a possibility that Napoleon could be killed in the war, and experts believe that the directory secretly hoped for that outcome.

On July 1, Napoleon landed in Egypt with a large army of around 40,000 fighters, and multiple ships. Napoleon's strategy was very well-defined and clear. First, they had to capture all the vital towns one by one, and soon they would have what was needed to defeat the British army. Alexandria was the first town the army came across, and they conquered it effortlessly. The next target town was Cairo, and Napoleon was determined to do more than conquer it. In addition to the army of fighters that he had brought, Napoleon also brought with him a large number of civilian scientists whose role was to establish a learning institution in Cairo. With the institution, Napoleon hoped to win people over through the provision of civilization in the form of education. Also, Napoleon constantly asserted that he was there to defend Islam and the Egyptian interest, and he soon gained their favor. While his assertions may have been true to some extent, Napoleon faced a lot of resistance, and rebellions soon began against his army.

The Battle of the Pyramids

This was the very first battle that Napoleon fought after his entry in Egypt, and it was against the Egyptian army. As stated, the Egyptians were not happy about the presence of Napoleon in the country, and they had immense reservation over his assertions that he was there in the best interest of the people. Initially, Napoleon did not have the desire to fight with the Egyptians, as his target was the British. However, when the clashes began, Napoleon led his army to war and had an easy win. Cairo was occupied immediately upon the defeat, and Napoleon took over the leadership of the same. Soon after the win, Napoleon wasted no time as he installed a new system of governance that ended feudalism and serfdom. Also, he imported some of the critical French structures, and soon, Egypt began adopting the new system of operations. Notably, Napoleon was not oppressive and was genuinely concerned about the needs of the people. It was his genuine resolve that with the new system, the people would be able to lead better lives.

The Battle of the Nile

With any conquest, there is undoubtedly bound to be some form of resistance, regardless of how beneficial the new system of governance is. The resistance is exactly what Napoleon faced when he took over Cairo. As soon as Napoleon landed in Egypt, the British got wind of what was happening, and they decided to stop him. While Napoleon had already captured Cairo, the one weakness that he had was that he could not command at sea. Therefore, he was hit by surprise when the British army attacked him, something that he had not anticipated. The British army came on strong and destroyed the entire fleet of ships that the French army had come with. Notably, the ships contained some of the most vital war resources that Napoleon has organized. Therefore, the sudden destruction imminently weakened his position.

The defeat was immense. Napoleon did not even have the resources to take his small surviving army back to France. Conceding defeat, Napoleon decided to March to Syria with the few survivors with the hope that he could get the Syrian army to take his side and drop any alliances that it may have had with the British army. The plan failed, and Syria even collaborated further with the British in an attempt to wipe out the small surviving team in its entirety. It was at this moment that Napoleon's will and courage were tested to the maximum. Even when he knew that he had potentially been defeated, Napoleon was still determined to prove a point, and he captured the first Syrian city he came across, which was known as Jaffa, and had 3,000 prisoners executed. He aimed at sending a message that he was still strong, with the hope that they would consider him an ally and help defeat the British. However, Syria was not welcoming in the least, and they responded by sending a 20,000-troop army to fight Napoleon. Luckily, Napoleon had already gotten wind of what was about to happen, and he quickly led his army back to Egypt before the British troops arrived. It was a lucky escape, and there is a very high likelihood that he would have been defeated and the remaining army wiped out had they stayed longer in Syria.

Leaving Egypt

Perhaps one of the most controversial decisions that Napoleon made was to leave Egypt after the embarrassing defeat. To many, Napoleon turned from a hero to a coward since he left his army behind, more or less abandoning them. Napoleon felt that he had lost everything, and even the rebels who had taken his side turned against him. To many, this seemed like the end of Napoleon and his leadership.

However, there was a clear motive and strategy behind this. During this period, Napoleon was unhappy with the French regiment and, to some extent, felt that they betrayed him since they did not send any backup the entire time he was in Egypt and Syria. He traveled back to France with one clear motive of taking over the government and saving his situation. Note that Napoleon traveled alone, which meant he knew the opposition he would face as well as possible elimination by the current government. However, Napoleon was unafraid and ready for any eventuality. During this time, his strong character started to show, affirming his legacy as one of the bravest people that ever lived. As it turned out, it was the defeat in Egypt that served as the defining moment for the onset of the Napoleonic wars.

CHAPTER 3

NAPOLEON AS THE FRENCH EMPEROR

The Coup of 18 Brumaire

When Napoleon left Egypt, he had mixed emotions—disappointment in the French government for seemingly abandoning him and the rest of the army, and anger due to the poor leadership displayed. He was determined to overthrow the government through a coup, although he was not the chief instigator. At the time, Sieyes, another disgruntled military official, felt that the government was not performing as it should, and he resolved to overthrow it. Napoleon found the situation already dire with the coup imminent, and he decided to capitalize on the situation.

Napoleon, being the skilled plotter and analyst that he was, thought about the many ways through which he could achieve the coup without getting killed in the process, and soon he had a clear strategy that he was sure would not fail. The first thing he needed to do was get the most powerful men in France on his side. These powerful men were the landowners in France, and their influence was immense. At the time, the landowners felt that their needs and rights were not being taken into consideration, and they were highly charged and motivated to attempt to change the system. Further, in the prior revolutions, a lot of lands had been stripped away from churches and many aristocrats and sold to the landowners. Since there was a possibility that the land would be stripped away from the landowners and restored to the rightful owners, these powerful people were living in constant fear, as having their land stripped would render them poor.

Napoleon took advantage of the situation and convinced them that he would be the one to instigate the changes they desired. Further, he assured them that as soon as he got into power, he would legalize the acquisition of the land, and no one would be able to take it away from them. Since his track record was solid and he had earned the admiration of many, convincing the people was quite easy, and he soon got the support he needed. Further, Napoleon drew a constitution that gave the landowners power and assured them that as soon as he was the emperor, the constitution would be legally binding. With such assurance, all the landowners and powerful people in France gave him their full support.

With the support of people of power, Napoleon was able to lead a coup that overthrew the government, making him the people's leader. The main government officials that were overthrown were the five directors who had advocated for Napoleon to lead the war against the British and who were greatly anxious that his popularity would soon work against them. Their fears soon came to pass as Napoleon took over the leadership and ousted them, much to the delight of all the citizens. Napoleon began acting fast, getting rid of all the former government officials and recruiting the ones that he wanted in power.

In 1804, the government officials, all of whom had been chosen by Napoleon, passed a law that made him the French emperor. Notably, Napoleon rejected the title of King, as he felt that it was too mainstream and not ambitious enough. Also, he wanted something different because he had always viewed himself as unlike any of the other leaders that had even been at the forefront of the French leadership. During the crowning, he was still married to Josephine, and she was consequently crowned empress.

In addition to his crowning, Napoleon extended his ambition to his family members, ensuring that a law was passed that recognized heirs and demanded that they come from his family tree. At that time, he did not have any children, but it was okay since there were other Bonapartes who could take a leadership role in case anything happened to Napoleon. The people were seemingly so happy about Napoleon's leadership that they supported his bid immensely. Of the official recognized votes that were cast, 3.5 million were in support of Napoleon's ideology, while only a meager 2,500 were against him. The support was a great stride on his part, as it showed the immense belief that the people had in him.

The Napoleonic Code

One of Napoleon's greatest legacies was the development of a modernized system of governance, one that still lives on and is referred to as the Napoleonic code. The Napoleonic code was established soon after Napoleon became the emperor, and it served as the alternative to the continental laws that had been in existence in the previous regimes. As is already evident, Napoleon was very vocal about feudal laws, and he was determined to eliminate them at all costs. Among the factors that led to the determination of changing the system was that Napoleon considered himself to be elite, and he could no longer stand the primitive governance that was majorly inclined toward oppressing the minority in society as well as taking advantage of their inferior status. Further, the fact that France did not have clearly defined laws meant that it was challenging to distinguish between right and wrong and the ordinary people did not even know how to seek justice for the wrongs they felt were being done against them.

Napoleon was also determined to change the existing laws that gave the feudal lords control over people's personal lives. As Napoleon noted, most ordinances, including marriage and family life, were significantly imposed upon by the kings, and the people seemingly had no control over any aspect of their lives. Worse, the laws kept changing each and every day, and this was how the lords managed to ensure that everything that they wanted came to pass. Whenever these lords desired anything to work in their favor, they changed the law, and the people had no option but to oblige. One example of such a situation was the lords passing a law that stipulated that the commoners had no right to refuse to work in the fields of their masters for free. Once it was passed, the commoners' suffering increased while the lords continued amassing wealth.

Napoleon began changing the legal system right after selecting a team of four that made up his jurists, and they came up with a set of legal doctrines and tenets that served as a replacement for the previous laws, which were vague. The jurists worked with Napoleon on the codes, and by 1801, they were done. It, however, took time for their publication, as Napoleon was still leading wars at the time and unsure if he could successfully impose the stipulations on the other nations. However, he commanded his jurists to begin educating the people about the changes they should expect from the new system of governance as well as the ways in which it would differ from the previous laws.

The primary tenets that formed the basis of the code were as follows:

1. Equality among all men

For the first time in history, a law based on rationale would be established, and it would be free from all the past prejudices that the people had already became accustomed to. One of the most significant aspects of the rationale was coming to terms with the fact that all men were equal and that no one had authority over anyone else. Through this code, Napoleon aimed at getting rid of all social classes, nobility, and the privileges that were only accessible to a small segment of the population.

Scholars assert that the desire to abolish the social classes had its basis from his childhood, given the fact that Napoleon was severely bullied due to his family's status and background. Therefore, Napoleon knew the effect that such groupings had on people, and he was determined to abolish them for good in his country. Going through school was definitely one of the toughest periods Napoleon experienced in childhood, and he was determined to save as many people as possible from such situations.

2. The law of persons

The law of persons dealt with all aspects of human rights and the protection of personality, guardianship, and relations. Napoleon knew how many people suffered from circumstances they could not control for the simple reason that it was what was widely accepted. People got accustomed to the worst of times, and they rarely made an attempt to change, as it was considered to be the usual and acceptable way of life. To overcome such laws, Napoleon required all laws that elevated some people while undermining others be disbanded entirely. A majority of the laws were in line with ownership of property as well as the guardian having absolute authority about what their children could and could not do. For instance, many people had arranged marriages, and the result was a life of dissatisfaction in a loveless marriage. According to Napoleon, every adult had the right to choose whomever they wanted to stay with and the person that they wished to marry without the interference of the broader public. Also, issues pertaining to divorce and marriage annulments would be handled by the relevant parties as they pleased, and nobody had the right to dictate what was supposed to happen in another person's life.

Further, customary and traditional laws would not have any influence on the new law, and moral justification would be based on its conformity to the decrees of reason and common sense. For example, beating up workers was considered to be a customarily regular occurrence. However, common sense dictates that all people are equal and should be respected, and the law would protect them henceforth. This is precisely what Napoleon was aiming at achieving.

3. The law of things

The law of things deals with the aspects relating to property rights, ownership of assets, and all issues relating to inheritance, succession, obligations, and any marriage settlements. Basically, all persons were allowed to own any property they acquired through legal means, and no person had the right to take it away from them on the basis of superiority or authority. Through this code, Napoleon ensured that all persons had equal rights and that all hardworking persons would get what they deserved. With the system, not only was there an increased sense of satisfaction among the people, but it also served as motivation. Eventually, France would be able to amass more resources.

Influence and Jurisdiction of the Napoleonic Code

The Napoleonic code was first introduced into the areas and countries that were under French control. These areas included Belgium, a few parts of Germany, Italy, Monaco, and Geneva. Later, Napoleon continued spreading the jurisdiction of the codes into the areas he gradually occupied and controlled, such as the

Netherlands, Switzerland, and Western Germany. Eventually, there were significant changes, and the people boasted of better living standards as soon as the code was in full effect, and Napoleon was determined to spread it wherever he went.

A few years after the first introduction, countries surrounding France were in awe at the level of development that accrued from the adoption of the code. So impressed were they that they voluntarily adopted the law and began changing their systems of governance. European and Latin American countries were the first to adopt this code willingly, and within no time, it had spread to multiple nations, some of which did not even have any level of acquaintance with France.

Currently, the Napoleonic code is still rife and alive in a significant section of the world. Napoleon had been amazed at the transformation to both his and other nations, and he always asserted that his real glory was not in the wars that he had fought and won, but the development of the civil code. True to his word, the code still lives, and nothing can destroy it.

Napoleonic Wars

The Napoleonic wars represent a series of battles that began when Napoleon took leadership of France, and they are considered to be the most defining battles Napoleon ever fought. It is not clear when the wars began exactly, but many historians believe that they commenced in 1803, a very short time after Napoleon succeeded in his coup (Connelly, 2012). The wars occurred at different times, and they are often categorized into five distinct coalitions.

The War of the Third Coalition (1803–1806)

The War of the Third Coalition was the first Napoleonic war that occurred after Napoleon's rise to emperor status. Before this war, there had been two other minor preceding wars—*the War of the First Coalition*, which occurred between 1793 and 1797, and *the War of the Second Coalition*, which took place between 1799 and 1801. These two wars were all in an attempt to defeat the French army, and they failed drastically. Ultimately, France and Britain reached a peace agreement in what is popularly known as the *Peace of Amiens*. This peace treaty involved Britain relinquishing all the control that it had previously taken on some of the French territory as well as other nations, such as Egypt. France, on the other hand, agreed to leave Italy and give up all the control it had on some of the cities therein. This peace treaty was among the highest points in time for all the nations, and it resulted in tranquility and respect that was previously unavailable. The peace would not last, as the War of the Third Coalition soon ensued.

In May 1803, two years after the peace treaty had been signed, hostilities suddenly erupted again. It was at this time that the Third Coalition was formed, comprising of England, Russia, Sweden, and Prussia. To a large extent, Napoleon was largely to blame for the formation of this coalition, as he had just recently started a military quest in Europe. Also, Napoleon had seemingly gone against the peace treaty by invading Italy, a factor that necessitated a coalition to stop him. At the time, Napoleon had already occupied a part of Switzerland and was at the time contemplating a re-invasion in Egypt. Even worse, he began disrespecting Britain because he felt that its army was weak. All of these nations were angered and they came together to stop him.

Notably, the fact that multiple nations formed a single coalition in an attempt to beat Napoleon affirms how strong he was. Napoleon was fearless, and he was ostensibly unaffected by the thought of the nations rallying against him. The fact that he had already strengthened the French army gave him confidence that he could defeat anyone, further affirming his position as one of the most robust and fearless leaders of all time.

How the Coalition Formed

The coalition formed to fight Napoleon took time, with the nations involved highly set and determined to ensure there was no way they lost. The first meeting was held in Vienna, and it was attended by some of the topmost and highly-sought leaders in the Russian and Austrian armies. The two nations were well aware of the power and strength Napoleon had, and they set aside 250,000 Austrian fighters and 180,000 Russians and began training them in preparation for the war. Both nations had the highest number of fighters, with the others comprised of the following:

» 100,000 Prussians
» 35,000 Germans
» 20,000 Neapolitans
» 5,000 Englishmen

- » 16,000 Swedes
- » 16,000 Danes

The teams began preparing with their various officials, and the leaders were already getting acquainted with each other in preparation of the Great War. When the training was complete, it was estimated that over 437,000 military members were selected to participate in the war. Around 100,000 military members from the Austrian army were kept at bay, and they would serve as reinforcement in case help was needed during the war.

Once the training was complete, the contingent got ready to advance and begin the war. Notably, there were military operations at both sea and land since the military knew that Napoleon was intelligent and would attack when they least expected. The military operations at sea were necessary since they would ensure that Napoleon had no way of reaching the British shores while the operation at land was meant to secure all the entry points that Napoleon could possibly use to attack. England played a major role in the operations at land and secured its border.

When the coalition formed, the major objective was to corner Napoleon at all sides and to ensure that he had nowhere to run to. Since the French army was concentrated in the north, the military coalition felt confident in defeating Napoleon if they attacked from all sides and cornered him at the middle. Unknown to them, Napoleon was not threatened in the least, and he was busy preparing his army.

The first army in the coalition to attack was the Austrian military. The army was made up of 72,000 strong fighters, and they invaded Bavaria. Napoleon heard about the invasion and left for Bavaria, where he defeated the army in no time. Defeated, the Austrian army was forced to retreat. As the war was taking place, the Russian army was heading to Bavaria to help the Austrians. When the commander heard about the defeat, they were no longer bold enough, and they resorted to retreating. Napoleon surged into the Russian territory and took the city of Vienna with no resistance.

The Austrian army soon converged with the Russian army and decided to approach and fight Napoleon as a single unit. Once they had prepared enough and recruited other fighters into the army, they approached Napoleon, and soon a battle erupted. Napoleon fought with gusto and easily defeated the combined army. The Russians and Austrians soon retreated, having suffered a crushing and severe defeat.

The outcome of this battle was better than Napoleon had even anticipated. After the Austrian army's defeat, the nation seemingly became more afraid of Napoleon since they had seen his strength. They swallowed their pride and agreed to sign a peace treaty with France. Napoleon wanted a number of Austrian territories handed over to him, and the Austrian government agreed with little resistance. Therefore, Napoleon became richer than he previously was and had the Austrians at his command. The Russians were against bowing to Napoleon and they continued with their military operations against him. While they did not attack him again at this point, it was clear that they would when another opportunity presented itself.

The War of the Fourth Coalition (1806–1807)

Soon after the defeat and surrender of the Austrians, a disgruntled coalition that largely consisted of the Prussians and the British was formed. The two nations had heard about the defeat of Napoleon, and they were actually adamant about approaching and fighting him. However, they knew the more Napoleon continued to be in charge and at the helm of the military, the more likely he was to take over more land and resources that belonged to the other coalitions. Ultimately, a total takeover was imminent, and Napoleon would be the overall king. None of the nations wanted this, and they came together to form another coalition to attempt defeating Napoleon again.

At the time of the convergence of the Third Coalition, Napoleon was still in Vienna, and he appeared to be quite isolated and alone. While the coalition thought the isolation was a sign of weakness and that they would have a very easy time defeating him, the truth was that Napoleon was strategizing about his next move; he knew there was an impending attack that could potentially be bigger and more serious than all the other battles he had fought. True to his thoughts, the Third Coalition struck, and Napoleon fought and won what is considered to be his most impressive battle in history.

Many historians have focused on the eventualities and nuances of this battle and the ways in which it shaped the reign of Napoleon. The one thing that stands out is that, unlike the many battles that Napoleon fought and won, in this case, he was not the instigator. The coalitions that were formed of the different nations were the aggressors, and all Napoleon did was retaliate and protect himself. Also clear is that Napoleon was fighting solely with the French army only while the coalitions had even more resources at their disposal, as they were behind many nations.

The War of the Fourth Coalition resulted in one major eventuality—Napoleon taking over the whole of Prussia. Note that Napoleon already knew there was an impending war. Being the fast and smart thinker he was, Napoleon decided to attack Prussia before the coalition attacked him so he could weaken them by taking over the entire nation. At the time, Prussia was still in the process of training with the other coalitions' armies, and it was their belief that Napoleon was doing the same. Consequently, being attacked caught them by surprise, and it was a very easy takeover on Napoleon's end. But he didn't stop there. He went on to fight and defeat Berlin, and in less than ten days, a total overthrow had already been completed. Just like what had happened in the War of the Third Coalition, Prussia conceded defeat, and they surrendered once again.

Napoleon knew better than to waste any time. At the time he was taking over the nations one by one, he knew that he had instilled some level of fear in all the other nations that were in opposition to him. Since he knew how easy it would be to defeat people who were already fearful of him, he immediately moved into

Russia. Note that the fact that Napoleon was winning the wars one after another does not mean his army was not getting harmed to some degree in the process. As with any war, his army also suffered a lot of casualties, and it took Russia by surprise as they expected the two battles to have weakened France to some extent. They were even more fearful of the French army as they did not know how they managed to succeed at the levels they did.

Fear was imminent in the Russian army; they continued to retreat as Napoleon moved in. With the retreat, Napoleon captured city after city, beginning with Warsaw. With each city captured, Napoleon replenished his horses and got even more volunteers to join his army. The need and human desire of being associated with the winning side saw very many young men join his army, and soon, Napoleon had one of the largest armies the world had ever seen. By the time he took over Warsaw, Napoleon had an estimated 60,000 good horses and hundreds of thousands of foot soldiers.

Napoleon continued to go deeper into Russia until he arrived at a place called Eylau, and the army set up camp. Winter had already set in so the army decided to stay since the unrelenting winter conditions were unforgiving outside. It was too cold to continue moving, and Napoleon had no intention of launching an offensive at the time. This may have been the one time Napoleon underestimated his enemies, thinking that no one would launch an attack in such extreme weather. He was wrong, and Russia charged unexpectedly, leading to one of the biggest and most extreme wars Napoleon ever fought.

The Battle of Eylau

As has been stated, Napoleon had no intention of fighting in the winter period once he took over some of the cities in Russia. However, Russia decided to launch an offensive, and Napoleon had no option but to retaliate as fast as possible. Naturally, fighting in the cold was not a good idea, and neither of the armies would be able to fight as efficiently as they would have had they undertaken the fight during a period with more favorable weather. Since Napoleon was already used to the wars, he knew that if the entire Russian army intercepted him, there was a chance he would be defeated. Thinking fast, he ordered part of the team to head west, away from the camp. This strategy was aimed at confusing the Russians into thinking the whole army was headed west, and the rest of the French team would have an easier time attacking them from behind.

Unfortunately, the Russian commander was also smart, and he knew that if the plan worked, there would be a very high likelihood that he would be cornered. The strategy also confused him, and he decided to fall back for a while so that he could read the French army and the exact tactics they could potentially use.

Seeing the Russian army fall back, Napoleon knew he had succeeded in scaring the Russians, which meant they would fight with little confidence. These were the chances Napoleon lived for. Therefore, he instructed his army to chase after the Russians and launch an attack. The army set off, chasing the Russians until they had no alternative but to turn back and fight.

Notably, the war was not as easy as Napoleon had anticipated. The Russians fought fiercely, and it was apparent that the French would not be able to take them down as easily. The war began at around 2:00 p.m., and both sides fought gallantly in the freezing weather. As the hours passed, neither army was surrendering, and the result was a bloodbath that had never been seen before. As the war raged on, the control of the city passed back and forth between the two sides, and both armies were determined to gain victory. When night approached, the Russian team decided to fall back, giving the French army a temporary belief and assurance that they had won the war.

The reality of the war was imminent the following morning. Thousands of fighters had been killed, with most of the dead being from the French army. Even worse, some of the soldiers who had been injured were freezing in the cold weather, and Napoleon was certain they would lose even more people to the weather. Of the over 100,000 military fighters that had set up camp, Napoleon had only around 45,000 able fighters. This number placed him at a serious disadvantage, considering the fact that the Russian army had around 67,000 troops. Napoleon was not shaken, and he immediately called for reinforcements. His many years of war had taught him that this was not the type of war that he could be confident was over. Russia was undoubtedly going to attack again.

True to his belief, Russia launched an attack early the following day. This was not the typical war where only swords and knives were used. Both armies had cannons and heavy machinery, and they did not shy away from using them on their enemies. The war was intense, and even the injured were commanded to join in. At that point, Napoleon needed all the help he could get.

As the war advanced, Napoleon realized that the Russians had stronger weapons than he even thought was possible. An entire team that had been sent out west to try and corner the coming Russian reinforcements came head-on with blazing guns, and they were wiped out in an instant. The loss of the gallant men presented even more trouble for Napoleon, and for the first time, he may have been shaken. The Russian army continued pushing deeper into Eylau and started showing signs of more strength and imminent victory. Napoleon stepped back to think and soon came up with the plan that managed to save his quickly weakening army.

First, the weather was very humid and the visibility was poor. If he could capitalize on this weakness, he would be able to turn the tables and France would have dominion over the Russians. Calling out to some of the fiercest fighters, Napoleon commanded them to try their best to take over the Russian machinery and weapons as he commanded the remaining army to fight the best they ever had at the field. The Russians realized that some of the French men were falling back, and they were confused, as they did not know whether it was a sign of surrender or if something else was going on. Even more confusing was the fact that the army on the ground was seemingly fighting even more strongly, and they did not know whether this team would fall back as well. Napoleon was counting on that confusion, as it would reduce the efficiency of the Russians by sending them mixed signals. True to his belief, the team that had broken off was able to take over all the major weapons as the troops had already been told that the French were apparently surrendering, which made them less vigilant. As soon as the French army took over the weapons, the bloodshed that followed among the Russian troops was unlike any other. Thousands more died and the Russians were weakened. Prior to that, Napoleon had called for reinforcement, and when they finally arrived, the Russian army was further massacred. By the time nighttime approached, the Russians had already conceded defeat, and the few military men that survived fell back. By 10:00 p.m. that night, the war was over.

The extent of the casualties and death was clear in the morning. The white snow was covered in blood, thousands of bodies scattered everywhere. Napoleon was saddened at the turn of events, and he asserted that he did not feel victorious. Of all the wars that he had been in, this was one that had cost him thousands of good men. In his words, Napoleon was disappointed at the extent of the massacre, and he felt that it had all been for nothing.

War of the Fifth Coalition (1809)

Napoleon's frequent victories against the coalitions that formed against him did not stop them from making more plans to defeat him. Austria was among the nations that were at the forefront of advocating for the wars, and they did not stop with the defeats they constantly suffered. During this period, many of the nations in the previous coalitions had already accepted and conceded defeat, and identified Napoleon as among those whom they would not be able to defeat easily. Therefore, they refrained from joining the coalition, leaving only Austria and the British in the fight against France.

When Napoleon heard that the Fifth Coalition was training and just about to attack him, he decided to change the tides and stop Austria before they were even strong enough to fight him. During the moments preceding the war, Austria came on strongly and even led an invasion into Bavaria. The army came out strong, and the few French militants that were there at the time were gradually forced to retreat. Napoleon got wind of what was happening and decided to stop the Austrian army once and for all. What followed was a smaller war known as the Battle of Eckmühl.

Battle of Eckmühl and Abensberg

The Battle of Eckmühl took place in April 1809, and it marked the beginning of the War of the Fifth Coalition. While Napoleon had heard there was a Fifth Coalition that was forming in an attempt to stop him, he was oblivious of the fact that Austria would attack that fast and by themselves. Markedly, the first attack against the French militants took place at a location where neither the French nor the Austrian army knew the surroundings well, which placed both groups at a disadvantage. Napoleon was determined to end the Austrian army, and he led troops in two different places. The first troops were reinforcements, and they helped beat the Austrian army. Napoleon knew the first group might have been just a distraction, so he led the other group west and in a different location, sure there would be other Austrian militants that would attempt to attack him therein. He was right, and he found an Austrian army on transit to France. The attack came as a surprise to the Austrians, and Napoleon defeated them easily. This war is known as the battle of Abensberg.

The aftermath of the war exhibited the severity by which the Austrian army had lost its militants. Over 12,000 Austrian militants were killed at the cost of just 5,000 French militants. Once again, Napoleon had established himself as among the greatest war leaders the world had ever known. It is alleged that this was among the most fulfilling wars that Napoleon had ever fought, rumored that he mentioned it was the finest of plans that he had ever conducted. After the victory, Napoleon moved into Austria and occupied the capital.

The victory against the Austrians made Napoleon more confident and significantly less empathetic against the Austrians. The result was the drafting of a peace treaty that is considered to be incredibly harsh. The treaty was meant to keep the Austrians grounded and also reduce their strength in case they ever decided to attack Napoleon again.

The main tenets of the treaty were as follows:

1. Austria had to surrender the Duchy of Salzburg to Napoleon. The city was the main access to the Adriatic Sea, and the surrender meant the Austrian army would be trapped in the country without a way out unless they went through the French. Therefore, it would be very difficult for them to interact with other nations that were against France, and they consequently couldn't use the sea as a means of transport anymore. This was the one tenet that really destroyed the

strength of the Austrian army, as without the sea they were stuck. Many other cities also surrendered, and Napoleon ensured the choice was strategic. The only cities he took over were the ones that had something to offer, since Napoleon knew he needed capital and resources more than anything else.

2. The Austrian army had to replace the able militants they had killed in the two wars. The indemnity was duly paid, and the Austrian army was reduced to just 150,000 men. With such a number, Napoleon was sure the Austrian army was crippled, and they could never engage in any other war unless they had the help of outsiders.

3. The Graz fortress, which was significant in the resistance against the French, had to be demolished. For a long time, the fortress inhabited persons who were against the French, and multiple coalitions against France were created therein. Therefore, Napoleon viewed it as a sign of resistance, and it had to go down. The Austrian army conceded, and the building was duly pulled down.

Austria had to disband their mode of governance and use the French continental system. The continental system largely encompassed a decree and allegiance to the French army through the avoidance of British trade. Therefore, Austria had to forbid any importation of British goods and the severance of any communication and interaction between them, including mail communication.

While the Austrians knew they had no choice but to abide by Napoleon's stipulations, they made one last attempt to eliminate him. On October 12, as Napoleon was preparing to sign the treaty with the Austrian officials, a young man requested an audience with the emperor so he could present a petition. The French army guarding Napoleon refused him and pushed him into the crowd. Later, Napoleon was watching a military parade when the French army noticed the same man pushing through the crowd and getting closer to where Napoleon was. Having been trained by the best, they knew there was a possibility the boy presented some level of threat, and they arrested and took him in. When they stripped him, they found a large knife hidden well in his coat. After a lengthy interrogation, Staps, the young man, revealed that he had the intention of getting close enough to Napoleon to kill him. Staps retorted that Napoleon had brought nothing but misery to Austria and that the lives of the common people were more miserable because of him.

Napoleon was a tough fighter, but the words of the young man struck a chord with him. So deep were the words that instead of being angry his life was threatened, he was willing to show him mercy. Attempting to create rapport and somewhat changing his impression to the young man, Napoleon asked him what he would do if he was pardoned. Categorically, Staps affirmed that he would come back and attempt to kill him at a later date. Napoleon was wise enough to know determination when he saw it, and he concluded that the young man was better off executed. The army shot him outside the palace in a public execution that drew wide and mixed reactions. In the end, people considered Staps to be among the bravest and most confident to ever challenge the French army, and to date, he is regarded as a martyr.

Crossing the Danube

The defeat of the Austrian army was both a blessing and a curse. It was a blessing in the sense that it affirmed Napoleon's character and status as a powerful person, and a curse in that it filled him with pride and a very false and misguided sense of security. Napoleon was determined to take up even more Austrian cities, with the first in line being Vienna. Note that, even though Austria had signed a peace treaty, they were very angry at the fact that Napoleon had taken over the majority of their cities, and they were still determined to take him out. As it turned out, the Austrian army was perhaps one of the forces that Napoleon seemingly underestimated too much, and it would affect him in more ways than he could even imagine.

Napoleon marched toward Vienna, expecting no resistance since he had already weakened the Austrian army and a peace treaty had already been signed. As Napoleon approached the city, he came face-to-face with the Austrian army, and he was sure he could defeat them easily. The only problem was that his intention was to cross a river, and if he responded to the Austrians by engaging in war, there was a possibility they would run into the nearby Bohemian nation.

The biggest problem with this occurrence is that Napoleon would undoubtedly be tempted to pursue them in a foreign land, and he knew of the possibility of it being a trap, which meant that he would be beaten in a foreign land. Also, Napoleon had not been in the nation prior, and he knew that this was a disadvantage on his end as it would give the Austrian army a competitive advantage and ultimately better chance of winning the war. Napoleon decided to be wise and avoid losing more of his army through another war as much as possible. Therefore, there was only one thing to do at this point. Napoleon decided to turn back and attempt to cross the river from a different location—a place known as the Danube.

As fate would have it, the Austrian army had already prepared for this eventuality, and they were waiting for Napoleon at the Danube. This army, led by an Austrian leader known as Charles, would be the most memorable and humiliating for Napoleon. Once the two armies met, it was evident that a war would soon erupt. By midday, the war had already begun, and both sides fought their best. By the end of the day, Napoleon won and pushed the Austrian army out of his way.

One major factor that made this war stand out from the other wars was the way in which the Austrian army had fought. Even though it was a win for Napoleon, it was not the typical war he had been used to. For starters, the Austrian army fought more gallantly than they ever had, and Napoleon's army was more overwhelmed than they ever had been in the past. This was a sign that Napoleon's performance was going down and an affirmation that the other armies were getting stronger by the day.

The battle drew a lot of mixed reactions from Napoleon's supporters and militants. Most of them were of the opinion that Napoleon would have performed much better had he chosen to destroy the Austrian army at the first chance he had, while others were unsatisfied with the manner in which the team had fought. However, Napoleon still maintained that he had managed to take over Vienna regardless, and the team prepared to start crossing the Danube as fast as they could.

Unknown to Napoleon, the resistance they had faced at the beginning was just a small portion of what the Austrian army had. Napoleon made his first major mistake during this time by believing that the biggest portion of the Austrian army had been left at Bohemia. The truth, however, was that the Austrian army had studied their defeats during all the other wars, and they knew how Napoleon operated. Napoleon had already gotten used to the idea that, whenever he won a war, the defeated nation fell back for a considerable amount of time. This time, he was wrong. The Austrian army had not even sent half of its army to the Danube the first time, and they had many more men awaiting Napoleon at the opposite side of the river. Napoleon knew there would be some form of resistance, although he expected them to be hidden and very few in total.

To affirm this, Napoleon sent out a few men to cross the river, and there was no counter-attack throughout the journey. For some reason, Napoleon's overconfidence clouded his sense of reason. When the men arrived at the opposite side, they only found a few Austrian militants who were not even interested in engaging them in a fight. Unknown to them, this was a strategic decision on the part of the Austrians. Well hidden in the hills, the Austrians wanted Napoleon to come with a sizeable army, as only then would they be able to weaken them. Killing a few French men would have no effect on Napoleon. However, if a large army was present, the Austrian army would use their newfound skills to kill as many as they possibly could, with the hope of bringing Napoleon to his feet.

When the first militants sent across were not attacked, Napoleon continued sending more men across, with the only challenge being that the bridge constantly broke as a result of the weight of the horses and strong men. Therefore, the militants would move in bits, allowing reconstruction whenever the bridge broke, and another team would cross. With time, the Austrians would realize the weakness with the bridges, and they chose to capitalize on the situation. Charles, the Austrian leader, came up with the decision to find a way of threatening the bridges so the French militants who had already arrived would be trapped alone and without the hope of receiving any reinforcements.

When Charles began to attack, Napoleon knew he could not hold them back. First, he was outnumbered by around three times in terms of weapons and militants. Also, the bridges were not yet complete, and he was sure that it would be a while before he received reinforcement. Therefore, the first instinct was to withdraw and escape from the imminent war. However, he decided to stay back and fight when he received the good news that the bridge was almost completed and the Austrian army had already launched an attack to French officials in the other parts.

Charles had learned from the previous wars, and he was slow to advance an attack. This time around, he was behaving like Napoleon by thinking about what he was doing keenly before actually implementing the strategies on the ground. Napoleon was still holding his ground, aware that he would lose if he chose to advance at the Austrian army first. He made a conscious decision to stay put and await the Austrian army to charge and attack him first. The advance was slow as each side was waiting on the other to charge, and soon, the Austrians realized the reason as to why Napoleon was not advancing was that he was greatly outnumbered. Therefore, it would be prudent to attack him at that point. A full-fledged battle soon ensued, and Napoleon fought quite impressively considering the fact that he was greatly outnumbered. At the end of the day, no one could claim victory, and the war raged on. At this point, the Austrian army kept breaking the bridges to prevent Napoleon from receiving reinforcements, and the battle at the river was also immense. Napoleon's army proved to be very effective as they were able to fight off the Austrians time and time again. However, it was not easy, and multiple times, the Austrian army was able to break the bridge. Nevertheless, the army that had already crossed at this point was handling the war well, and Napoleon was on the verge of winning.

Napoleon kept making the same mistake of underestimating the Austrian army even after the heavy fight. Similarly to what he had been accustomed to in the past, he expected the army to fall back and concede defeat as the dark approached, which would give him the chance to continue with his mission of taking over Vienna. However, the Austrian army was as strong as ever, and they fell back to strategize on how they would carry out attacks the next day.

The following morning, the war resumed and this time, Napoleon was the one who launched the attacks. The procedure was similar to what had happened the previous day. The bridge would be restored upon falling, allowing more French troops to cross and the process repeated in the case it fell. The major challenge, just like before, was that the Austrian army was also breaking the bridge purposefully, and the fact that they held a very protective and strong front meant the French had a very difficult time rebuilding it in the first place. As the war raged on, more troops entered to help Napoleon, and the Austrians were surprisingly better at war than anyone ever thought was possible. The battle was anyone's, as both armies took the lead at different points of the day.

Napoleon's army started relaxing when they realized they were receiving more reinforcement with every successful crossing of the troops. This was a mistake on their side, and it gave the Austrians a chance to do two major things that changed the course of the war. First, two large ships were commissioned to hit and break the bridge, and Charles commanded his entire army to engage in the war. The ships set sail and hit the bridge, breaking it at multiple points that would take days—even weeks—to successfully repair.

Even though some of the Austrian militants perished in the accident, it was worth it because it gave them the competitive edge that changed the course of the war. When the French army realized what had happened, they suddenly started panicking, resulting in making more mistakes and having decreased confidence in their skills. Ultimately, the French were pushed back, and they retreated, resulting in Napoleon's first defeat ever.

This battle was revolutionary since it resulted in three major eventualities:

1. First, the Austrians became even more confident they could stand their ground, having defeated a man that everybody considered to be undefeatable. There is something about confidence and the joy of winning an impossible task, and the result was that the Austrian people became even more confident in their militants as thousands more joined the army. Therefore, Austria was able to create an army that was unlike any other in the history of the country.
2. Second, the news about the defeat of Napoleon

spread all over the world. Nations far and wide heard about what had ensued in Vienna, and a new wave of revolution was imminent. As you may have figured, Napoleon had thousands of opponents, and his defeats restored their enthusiasm that they, too, could beat him and regain the cities that had fallen under French rule. Simply put, Napoleon was about to face the biggest revolution the world had ever seen.

3. Third, the defeat broke Napoleon. There was something about being the best, then suffering defeat from those least expected as being capable of victory over him. For the longest time, Napoleon had considered the Austrian army to be a non-threat, and he was sure that they could never beat him. In the course of the previous coalitions, Napoleon had defeated the Austrians more than five times, and to suffer a defeat from them was very humiliating. Further, he knew that the news about the defeat would spread and that all the people who had confidence in him would lose it, and his ego was severely bruised.

This War of the Fifth Coalition changed Napoleon like no other battle did. Many people assert that Napoleon was egotistic and that is why he was never able to recover from this defeat. As the upcoming wars showed, this was the beginning of the end of Napoleon.

War of the Sixth Coalition (1813–1814)

The War of the Sixth Coalition took place between March 1813 and May 1814 in Europe, and it is considered to be a war of liberation in Germany. The War of the Sixth Coalition was largely influenced by the War of the Fifth Coalition, where the different military associations had regained new confidence regarding the strength of Napoleon and their ability to beat him in the different wars. As soon as Napoleon was defeated by the Austrians, there was increased confidence from his opponents, and they were ready to come up to him once again and regain all that they had lost from him. In the previous wars, Napoleon had taken over many cities in different countries, and they were all ready to regain them back. Largely, this War of the Sixth Coalition was between the Prussians, Austrians, Portugal, Spain, Sweden, Germany, and many other small nations that had at one point clashed with the French army.

There are a number of battles that took place involving the sixth coalitions. Some of the notable ones included the following:

Battle at Lützen (May 2, 1813)

The battle of Lützen was the first battle Napoleon fought soon after his defeat by the Austrians in the Fifth Coalition. During this time, Napoleon was still embarrassed and angered by his defeat, and he was determined to reclaim his legacy as the greatest warrior that ever lived. Napoleon had lost many troops in the previous war and enemies knew it would take quite a while before he was able to rebuild it. However, Napoleon was a master at his craft, and he still retained the love and admiration of quite a number of his countrymen. With love and support, Napoleon was able to build back an army faster than his enemies could have fathomed, and soon he had a sizeable number.

Once Napoleon was sure that his men were well trained and could fight, he sought to advance into the north of Germany with the aim of capturing and seizing Danzig. This time around, he knew a lot of nations were already rallying against him, and the fact that he had already suffered massive defeat meant their confidence was over the top. Therefore, he could not afford to underestimate any of them. He considered all possibilities and potential eventualities, planning carefully until he was sure about what he was doing. First, he would concentrate the army at a location called

Erfurt and advance on any attackers from any direction they came from. Also, the army would travel in groups so they could offer some form of reinforcement in case the main army needed it.

As the French army was advancing toward Germany, around 100,000 men made up of the Prussians and Russians intercepted them. Napoleon had already learned from his previous battle, and he used the first group as bait to see if there was any other army that would attempt to attack them from elsewhere. When the battle began, Napoleon realized there was no other attacker, and he drove the entire army into fighting off the Prusso-Russians. The attackers were defeated, and the Napoleon who won battles was back. Both armies had casualties in excess of 20,000, and the Prusso-Russians felt more pressure compared to Napoleon since they had fewer militants. Napoleon knew there would be more attacks, and he was ready to keep up the winning strides.

Battle of Bautzen (May 20–21, 1813)

Napoleon's victory in the Battle of Lützen sent both the Russian and Prussian armies into a frenzy. Napoleon knew the win would be short-lived and the combined army would make advances at him again in the attempt to defeat him. Therefore, he began preparing his army and had more men recruited so they could replace the thousands of militants that had been killed in the previous battle. The recruit went well, and soon enough, Napoleon had a well-stocked army.

Among the factors that always gave Napoleon an upper hand was able informants who kept him in the loop about each and every single thing that was happening in his country and nearby countries. Through such informants, Napoleon learned that a defensive line had already been formed by the combined army of the Russians and Prussians, which meant they had also resorted to recruiting more militants and fighters. So advanced was the military that they formed lines that were seven miles long. Immediately, Napoleon knew he could not wait for them to attack and that he was better suited to lead the advance. As had been apparent in the other fights, the show of increased confidence in one army served as a threat to the others, and Napoleon needed to make the enemies know that he was not afraid of them in the least.

On May 19, Napoleon slowly advanced with his army right to where the Prusso-Russian army was. As soon as he arrived, he realized he had no match. All throughout, Napoleon had the notion that the combined army would have more than 150,000 militants. However, the number was much less, so much that he was almost disappointed. The total number of his opponents did not amount to more than 96,000 men, while Napoleon had virtually double the number. The overestimation was, however, in his favor. Right there, Napoleon was convinced that it would take him less than a day to defeat the combined army.

Napoleon soon set his plan in motion. Since they had the numbers, they would attempt to surround their opponents, weakening them on every side before killing as many as possible. By surrounding the enemies, all Napoleon wished to achieve was preventing the escape and retreat of most of the fighters, which would make the combined army have a harder time recruiting more soldiers in case they desired to attack him at a later date. The fact that both countries had engaged in so much battle meant that recruiting was not an easy process, and they could not get militants and fighters as quickly as they would have been able to in the past.

By noon, Napoleon had sufficiently and strategically placed his fighters, and he got ready to attack. The French artillery fire opened at around 3:00 p.m., and Napoleon ensured that he was doing the minimum. By avoiding significant progress, Napoleon hoped he would weaken the Allied forces significantly, ultimately keeping them pinned and ensuring they had very little energy left to fight a full-fledged war as soon as Napoleon decided to attack. His plan worked, and by 6:00 p.m., his opponents were getting tired. Throughout the day, they had hoped that Napoleon would fully advance towards them, and when he failed to do so, they were confused. Napoleon counted on that confusion, and as dark fell, his army was able to take their positions unnoticed around these Allied militants.

At dawn the following day, Napoleon resumed with his slow advances, doing the bare minimum. When he was confident that his entire army was in position, he then began the full-fledged attack. Had there not been a violent thunderstorm, Napoleon would have defeated the military more than he did on that day. Many militants were able to escape, contrary to Napoleon's desire to have most of them killed so as to prevent the probability of another attack from happening in the near future. The rain, coupled with a few mistakes on the side of the French militants, allowed most of his opponents get away intact, making sure they would undoubtedly launch another attack soon.

Battle of Dresden
(August 26–27, 1813)

The Battle of Dresden occurred two months after the previous major battle of Lützen, and it marked Napoleon's last victory in Germany. In the previous war, Napoleon had won, although far from his terms. While his desire was to have killed as many opponents as possible, rain and mistakes from his team members ruined his plans, and most of his opponents escaped. The Allied army spent two months recruiting and training more fighters, and by August, they had already doubled their first number. Napoleon, on the other hand, may have been a little lax when it came to the recruitment process, as he had 120,000 militants in comparison to the 170,000 troops that belonged to the Allied army.

At the time of the war, Napoleon was held at Dresden, and the Allied army knew if they could capture the area, they would have the upper hand since it was the French's center of operation. Not only did Napoleon's army train there, but the entire supply of their fighting weapons was located there. Therefore, successfully attacking it would render Napoleon helpless, and they could potentially defeat him. Napoleon had proceeded to Dresden with only a few men, no more than 20,000.

However, Napoleon had formed a robust military base and he knew that reinforcements would arrive in the minimum time possible in the event he was attacked. When he learned of the vast army of Allied troops approaching Dresden, reinforcements were called upon immediately.

The loyalty of Napoleon's army was evident after the call for reinforcement. The rest of the military had been far off in France, over 190 kilometers away. As these were the on-the-ground fighters, they had to cover the entire distance on foot. The army was estimated to be 190,000, and it resulted in what is still one of the most significant marches in history. Within four days, the militants had arrived.

While the French army had been on their way, the Allied army was busy making fortifications so they would be safer when the war began. Napoleon knew the fortifications would hinder him from achieving a proper attack, but he could not do anything until reinforcements arrived.

The Allied army was the first to attack, and Napoleon was fortunate that all the reinforcements had already arrived at the time. This army was very strategic, and they used heavy weapons and cavalry in the attempt to intimidate Napoleon as much as they could. Napoleon, however, was lucky there was a lot of mud and some rain, which affected the other side's heavy weapons by making them relatively ineffective in the war. One of the most significant mistakes this army had made was to lay out the weapons openly, and they soon realized that a good number of them were not even working anymore. Napoleon, therefore, had a considerable advantage.

The leading French army began attacking at around 7:00 a.m., hours after the opponents had already started the attack. Napoleon had realized that the opponents' weapons were problematic, and he opted to wait until they had used up most of them so he could attack and destroy them with little resistance. His plan worked. By the time he began the attack, the Allied were already frustrated, and they could not fight as effectively as the French were doing. Ultimately, Napoleon defeated them, killing more than 30,000 of their men while he lost less than 10,000 himself.

A shift of events would soon occur when Napoleon became ill right after the victory. So sick was he that he could not lead his army anymore, and he sent the corps commanders to pursue the fleeing Allies. This was not a wise decision, and the military faced a massive battle.

The Allied fought with skill, and the French army was severely defeated. Ultimately, the win at Dresden was canceled out, and the French could no longer claim victory.

The Battle at Leipzig, a.k.a. Battle of the Nations (October 16–19, 1813)

The Battle at Leipzig is also known as the Battle of the Nations, and it is the most massive Napoleonic war that ever took place. Prior to the First World War, the Battle of the Nations was singlehandedly the largest battle in history, involving more than half a million men. The war involved separate armies that were coordinated and fighting toward the single purpose of ousting Napoleon. These men consisted of the Russians, Prussians, Austrians, and the Swedes. Collectively, over 1,300 heavy guns were available and with the opposition troops while Napoleon had 717 guns.

While it is clear that Napoleon was at a disadvantage, it is important to realize he had no supporters and was fighting on his own. Therefore, coming up with 717 guns while a combination of more than five countries had 1,300 is an illustration of the extent of the resources that were available to Napoleon and how well prepared he was as a leader and militant.

Napoleon already knew the number of men that were intent on attacking him, and he knew the battle would not be like any other he had ever fought. Not only was he outnumbered by more than double, but his weapons also could not measure up with those of his opponents. Napoleon had already been in a similar situation at a previous battle, and he knew the best thing to do was to attempt to fight the nations one by one before they came together to fight as a single unit. Thus, he had to instigate the fight right before his opponents were even aware or anticipating an attack. There was only one major flaw in the plan. Attacking the different armies independently meant that all of his commanders had to act independently and attempt to provide the skilled leadership and quick decision-making that Napoleon usually accomplished. This presented a problem since the marshals and commanders available were not nearly half as good as Napoleon. Further, Napoleon had maintained an autocratic system of leadership, which meant he would tolerate no competition, and he had done little to train the marshals to be as good as him. Despite the weakness, the battle had to be fought.

On the first day of the battle, Napoleon sent a section of his army to the north at a place where he had heard a part of the Prussian army was advancing from. The Prussians were on their own, and the French army had a very high chance of fighting and winning that day. For the more substantial part of the battle, the Prussians were defeated and had even started retreating. This short-lived defeat gave Napoleon some sense of pride and even undue overconfidence, and he began making mistakes. First, his army already had clear instructions pertaining to how they were expected to proceed. Napoleon kept changing the instructions, and soon the army was confused.

It was while the instructions were still relatively unclear that the Allied nations had a chance of getting together, and they formed a front that was too much for even a confident and qualified man such as Napoleon. Napoleon kept redeploying reinforcements to help the trapped troops, and even they did not help. The Allied army was too strong. Withdrawing and pulling out was not an option since the major bridge that connected the French to Leipzig kept getting destroyed by the thousands of French men crossing. The army was trapped, and their best chance of survival was staying put and fighting off the attackers by all means. The fight waged on, and at the end of the first day, Napoleon had lost 73,000 men, compared to the 50,000 men that belonged to the Allied nations.

The battle of Leipzig marked the first occasion where Napoleon was clearly and indisputably defeated. This defeat was different from all others in the following sense:

» The Austrian victory in 1809 was more of a stalemate and not a clear win, and the supposed win was soon reversed when Napoleon beat the army in the war of Wagram in the same year.

» The Russian victory in 1812 was caused by Napoleon's flawed strategy of fighting and not the actual defeat of the army on the field.

The battle of Leipzig ended in Napoleon losing troops and being defeated in the field, something that had never happened before. At this point, Napoleon had no will to fight anymore, and he turned back and fled to Paris.

The Battle of Paris (March 1814)

The Battle of Paris signified the first major war that Napoleon was involved in right after his defeat in Leipzig. Just like the other war, the Allies of the Sixth Coalition were more charged than ever following the defeat of Napoleon, and they were determined to make him fall to his knees. Despite the defeat, Napoleon still held a number of cities in Germany, Israel, and across other small countries. The Sixth Coalition was not only determined to take back all the cities but aimed at ensuring that Napoleon abdicated and stepped down from power for good.

The coalition forces recruited more militants and troops, and it is estimated they had about 400,000 once they started marching toward France. The French army, on the other hand, was down to less than 70,000 troops, for multiple reasons. First, the people were no longer confident about Napoleon's ability to lead and win a war. As such, there were not as many volunteers as there typically had been in previous years. Further, the fact that Napoleon fought on his own meant there were even less available strong men in his country that could join and fight in the war.

Napoleon may have been disappointed and even had his ego bruised in the previous war, but he was not about to watch his city be taken away from him while he did nothing. Therefore, he organized the available troops and got ready for war. Notably, Napoleon had a big advantage over the other forces, which was that he was both fighting on a friendlier ground and that he was at home. He was able to prepare effectively and strategically place the army at positions that would give him the best advantage and a higher chance of succeeding.

Using this advantage, Napoleon was able to defeat the coalition forces that preceded the attack as they came independently. As more reinforcement came in, it was clear there was nothing much he could do, and a defeat was imminent. However, Napoleon still stood his ground and fought the armies as they arose, one after the other. The French citizens were immensely scared when the war was brought into their country, as it had been more than 400 years since a foreign army had entered France. Napoleon was counting on a revolution, which would have seen the populace stage a war against the attackers, and he hoped that maybe that would have helped them win the war. However, the coalition knew about this probability, and they sent ravens to the people with the assurance that none of the ordinary persons would be harmed as long as they kept away from the war. According to the coalition commander, the armies were against Napoleon and not the French people. This assurance, coupled with the fact that most people had already lost hope in Napoleon, resulted in an unnatural peace and calmness, and the commoners stayed away from the war. At this point, the defeat of Napoleon was imminent.

The coalition stayed true to their assurance, and they purposefully drove Napoleon as far away from the city as possible. Ordinary people were safe, as none of them would be harmed during the war. Soon, the marshals and the rest of the army surrendered when they finally realized they could not fight the coalition. Napoleon heard about the surrender and was angered. His first instinct was to turn back and lead the army that was with him to the city and fight, but the marshals and troops were already done. None of them were willing to fight anymore, and they pleaded with Napoleon to abdicate. On April 4, Napoleon finally abdicated in favor of his son. However, the coalition would not allow him to act on his terms, and they ensured that Napoleon abdicated unconditionally. The terms of the abdication spelled out that he would not be killed and would be exiled to the Island of Elba. These conditions were settled in a treaty known as Fontainebleau, and the War of the Sixth Coalition was finally over.

CHAPTER 4

THE FALL OF NAPOLEON

N apoleon was successful for very many years. Unfortunately, his tenure came to an end when he was defeated and overthrown from power in 1815. The downfall began soon after the defeat at the Battle of Paris, a fight that forced him not only to retreat but also to proceed to exile.

Napoleon's Exile to Elba

The Allied powers declared that Napoleon was the obstacle toward the restoration of peace in France. According to the treaty of Fontainebleau, Emperor Napoleon was to be taken by the Allies to exile in Elba, which was an island in the Mediterranean Sea. The Allies gave Napoleon sovereignty over the island and allowed him to retain the term *emperor*. While this may have seemed like a good deal, considering the fact that Napoleon was in exile, the truth is that Napoleon felt much disrespected and distressed. Initially, he had the dominion of over 70 million people, and the island only had 12,000 people. So distressed was he that he even attempted to take his life using pills he had obtained in Moscow after his defeat from the Prussians. However, the pills did not work, and Napoleon survived.

Napoleon was not imprisoned on the island, and he had chosen it as the preferred location for his exile. Not only did the island have crystal clear waters, but it was also very rich in minerals. Despite the fact that Napoleon initially felt disrespected and did not even want to stay there, he decided that the best he could do was to lead the people to the best of his ability, and maybe someday he would have the chance to go back to France and reclaim his title.

Gradually, the island became more united than it ever had been in the history of its existence, and a lot of developments took place at the time. To date, Napoleon is known as the only leader who managed to unite the territory, and it fell apart as soon as he left. To many observers, it seemed like Napoleon had the best life and was content with retirement. However, Napoleon was just strategizing, and it would only be a matter of time before he came up with an excellent plan to get himself out of that place.

Napoleon proved to be strong and dedicated to the military. After some few months in exile, he created a small army and navy, which affirmed his position as a born militant. Also, he led in the development of the iron mines, watched over the construction of new roads, and issued declarations about upcoming methods of agriculture. Being very vocal on civilization, Napoleon also revamped the island's legal and education system.

Napoleon knew the importance of being in the light and seeking as much information as he could concerning what was happening around him. Despite there being guards who constantly watched him, Napoleon was not in isolation, and he had access to multiple letters, newsletters, and publications from all over the world. It was while he was reading one of the newsletters that he got to learn about the demise of his ex-wife Josephine. The first empress had committed suicide under unclear circumstances, and Napoleon was greatly troubled. He locked himself in a room, wept, and did not leave for two whole days. Evidently, he still loved her very much. Napoleon's wife and his son went to Austria to seek refuge, and they were safe. Surprisingly, Napoleon was not as concerned about the current wife as he had been about Josephine. After learning about her death, Napoleon made up his mind to escape.

Napoleon's Escape from Exile

Napoleon knew there were guards whose role was to watch over him and report any deeds and misdeeds that he may have been involved in to the Allied coalition. Therefore, Napoleon had learned to be very careful in words and deeds, and he planned the escape alone. Since the army saw nothing suspicious in anything he did, they did not find it awkward when Napoleon began organizing an army, and they thought that he was merely performing his duty as the emperor of the island. Unknown to the guards was the fact that Napoleon had maintained secret communications with some of the marshals in France, and they awaited his return. The communications were dangerous to the coalition and were a time bomb, which had since relaxed.

Napoleon had intended to plan the escape slowly but soon changed his mind when he learned there were plans to move him from Elba to another island in the South Atlantic. The coalition had decided on the move, owing to the fact that an uprising had started against their rule, and they were worried that Napoleon would soon get help from his people if he continued staying in

Elba, which was near France. Therefore, the only option was to move him further, leaving the people destitute. Napoleon could not allow this to happen, and the fact that he was sure of support back at home gave him the motivation he needed to run away.

At first, Napoleon desired to run unnoticed. Later, he decided the best course of action was to act boldly, and he even began telling more people about his intentions. So bold was he that he even met up with some of the Elba officials and bid them goodbye. He left with his army that consisted of around 1,150 troops that he had trained, and soon he was back in France. Having carried out sufficient intelligence, Napoleon was sure he would arrive in France faster than any plan would be devised against him. True to his words, this was exactly what happened. The people heard about the heroic escape and were elated. Within no time, he had the support of the French as well as the army he had left behind. The emperor of France was back.

On March 13, the powers of the Congress of Vienna declared that Napoleon was a fugitive. After about four days, the coalition army made up of Great Britain, Russia, Prussia, and Austria each provided 15,000 soldiers to end the rule of Napoleon.

Napoleon arrived in Paris on March 20 and ruled for a period that is now referred to as a hundred days. By early June, Napoleon had about 200,000 armed forces. He planned to attack oncoming Britain and Prussian armies. The armed forces of Napoleon attacked the coalition troop of Britain and Prussia, and the Duke of Wellington and Prussian Prince Blücher finally started preparing for one of the most defining battles—the Battle of Waterloo.

Battle of Waterloo

The Battle of Waterloo took place on June 18, 1815, in Belgium, part of the United Kingdom of the Netherlands. At the time, Napoleon had been back to power from March 1815, and many states were against him. Therefore, they formed the Seventh Coalition to mobilize their armies and attempt to defeat the French. Two major armies made up the coalition, headed by the Duke of Wellington from Britain and Field Marshal Blücher from Prussia. This battle turned out to be among the most decisive engagements of the Waterloo campaign and signified the beginning of the end for Napoleon.

The war was orchestrated by the British and Prussian militants, and it is clear they had a well-defined plan as to how they would beat Napoleon. The armies of the Duke of Wellington and Blücher were close to the northeast border of France, and Napoleon had already confirmed that they were approaching him. At this point, Napoleon had learned to be more vigilant, and he refrained from assuming his opponents were harmless. He knew the only way to stop them was early enough while they were still in their distinct countries and before they came together to fight as a unit. His plan worked.

Napoleon successfully attacked the large Prussian army at the Battle of Ligny with his main force on July 16 while another portion of the French army attacked the Anglo-Allied army at the battle of Quatre Bras. The defeat of the Prussians made the Duke of Wellington withdraw north to Waterloo on July 17, but Napoleon was not done with him. He sent his forces to pursue the Prussians that had withdrawn parallel in good order to the Duke of Wellington. This led to the separate Battle of Wavre with Prussian guards. The Duke of Wellington prepared another battle on Mont-Saint-Jean escarpment on July 18, where he managed to attack France together with the support of the Prussians, who had arrived as reinforcement at the time.

The sudden attack took a massive toll on Napoleon. While it is not clear what exactly led to poor performance, the French army was beaten thoroughly. Some schools of thought attribute the defeat of Napoleon to be a result of two critical things:

1. First, Napoleon had been fighting alone and without the help of any other nation ever since the First Coalition was formed against him. Therefore, while the other armies always had new, robust, and much healthier militants, Napoleon was always using the same fighters for all his wars. At some point, these militants were bound to get exhausted. The poor performance was illustrated at this battle.

2. There was a loss of confidence about how long Napoleon could keep fighting his enemies. In as much as he had won multiple battles, the coalitions kept cropping up year after year, and without the support of any other nation, Napoleon could not fight them off forever.

With these two significant shortcomings, Napoleon decided to run away and re-strategize. The powers at the Congress of Vienna heard about the escape and declared Napoleon a fugitive. On March 13, 1815, the United Kingdom, Russia, Austria, and Prussians mobilized their armies to defeat France. Napoleon had known that his attempt to stop his opponents from invading France had failed. The only way for Napoleon to succeed was to destroy the existing coalition forces. Just like before, his plan was to attack them before any coalition had materialized. Previously, Napoleon had succeeded in destroying an alliance in Brussels, which made him confident that he could also drive off the British back to the seas and knock Prussians out of the war.

Napoleon knew that, by being a fugitive and hiding from his enemies, he would get time to recruit men and train them before engaging in the war. The British Commander Arthur Wellesley, the Duke of Wellington, knew that Napoleon was up to something, and they had to counter the threat of a surprise attack and potentially envelop coalition armies. Napoleon was determined to begin by stopping the British to ensure that they would not succeed. To achieve this, Napoleon started by spreading false information about the supply of the Duke of Wellington's chain being cut, hence giving the impression that the Duke of Wellington's deployment would be delayed. When the news reached the Duke of Wellington, he began panicking and could not proceed with his plans of attacking France. It would be a while before he realized that this was false information and that Napoleon was counting on the delay to buy more time and raise an army.

Napoleon raised an army of about 300,000 men by June. He divided his army into three—the right wing (commanded by Marshal Ney), the left wing (commanded by Marshal Grouchy), and the reserve under his own command. The three groups would potentially fight independently, although they were required to remain close and support each other. On June 15, France secured central position between the armies of the Duke of Wellington and Field Marshal Blücher, hoping this would prevent them from coming together and that he would be able to destroy the Prussians army first, then the army of the Duke of Wellington.

The Duke of Wellington got to know about the French's plans late in the night of June 15. On June 16, he received a dispatch from the Prince of Orange, meant to give him reinforcement against Napoleon. At the time, he did not know that Napoleon had already recruited thousands, and he expected any battle with the French to be an easy and effortless win. Napoleon was one who was always unpredictable, and when he advanced, the Duke of Wellington was shocked. Not only was the pace faster than he expected, but he also had a more massive army than the opponents expected. The Duke of Wellington ordered his army to concentrate at the Quatre Bras when the Prince of Orange was holding the tenuous position against the left French wing that was led by Marshal Ney. Napoleon had three divisions in his army and had selected the bravest to lead them. The Duke of Wellington knew Marshal Ney, and he was confident the battle would not be as easy as he anticipated.

Ney's instructions were to protect the crossroads of Quatre Bras, which was close enough to where Napoleon was. Therefore, he could consult Napoleon when necessarily. The crossroads were held lightly by the Prince of Orange, who repelled Ney's initial attack and was driven back by a large number of the French troops. The Duke of Wellington later arrived and drove Ney back, hence securing the crossroads by evening.

Napoleon led his division with vigor and strength, attacking and defeating the Prussians at the Battle of Ligny, using the right wing of his army and without any help from the other divisions.

While Napoleon was celebrating his win, it did not occur to him that this was a trap and the Prussians were just meant to be a distraction. The Prussian withdrawal from Ligny went uninterrupted and unnoticed by the French, and some did not move out until the following morning. Therefore, while Napoleon thought they were still around and the battle would continue, the truth was that they had left to a different location. Most of the Prussians did not participate in the war, a strategy that was meant to ensure they were strong enough for the other upcoming fights. The Prussian withdrawal from Ligny was prior to the Duke of Wellington's position at Quatre Bras. Napoleon, with his other reserves, joined Ney's at Quarter Bras on June 17 to attack the Duke of Wellington, but they found the location empty. The French army was dismayed and shocked, and they attempted to pursue the Duke of Wellington's withdrawing army into Waterloo. However, they were unable to as the bad weather made it impossible to maneuver the hills. The delay would later have a very negative impact on Napoleon, as it gave the Duke of Wellington the upper hand to prepare for the impending French attack.

Napoleon ordered Grouchy, who led the right wing, to follow the disappearing Prussians with 33,000 men since he was confident that if the Prussians met with the Duke of Wellington, they would fight together. However, Grouchy was too late to prevent the Prussian army from reaching Wavre, as he had started pursuing them late and had been uncertain about the direction of the Prussians because of the vagueness of the orders he was given by Napoleon. The Duke of Wellington arrived at Waterloo with the main Napoleon army following. Blücher was gathering his army in Wavre. The Duke of Wellington was assured by Blücher that the Prussian army would support him. The Duke of Wellington decided to take the ground and battle at Waterloo.

The Armies

There were three armies that participated at Waterloo—Napoleon's army, the Duke of Wellington's army, and a Prussian army under Blücher. Napoleon's army was composed of central veterans who were experienced and devoted to their emperor. There were many units that were guarded by the soldiers they didn't know since the soldiers were assigned units as they presented themselves. The French army was forced to march through rain and coal mud to Waterloo. Little food was available to the soldiers. Nevertheless, the veteran soldiers maintained their loyalty to the emperor.

The Duke of Wellington had very weak, inexperienced, and poorly equipped militia. All the

British soldiers were regular soldiers, and some of them were in peninsular war. Most of the troops in the coalition were inexperienced. Many of the professional soldiers in the coalition army had fought with the French military, which made them weak to some extent and worn out. The Duke of Wellington also lacked enough heavy cavalry, which gave Napoleon the upper hand. Despite this lack, the Duke of Wellington was brilliant, and he moved to lead the assault.

The Duke of Wellington stationed a further 17,000 troops at a nearby location who were under the Prince of Orange's younger brother, Prince Fredrick of Netherlands. The role of the forces was to safeguard any possible wide detaching movement by the French forces and to act as a rearguard if the Duke of Wellington was pushed and in case he needed help.

The Prussians were in the process of reorganization in the former reserve regiments, and the volunteers in the war of 1813–1814 were in the process of being absorbed. The Prussian army had the best professional leadership in its organization since they had came from schools that were developed for military purposes. The system contrasted with the vague orders issued by the French army, giving them an upper hand in the war. The system ensured that the three-quarters of the Prussian army was to participate in the field for about twenty-four hours. Although they were defeated in the battle of Ligny, the Prussian army was able to realign its supply and intervene in the Waterloo battlefield within forty-eight hours.

The Battlefield

Waterloo was positioned firmly, having long ridges running east to west and perpendicular to the main road of Brussels. There was an elm tree that was centered near the Duke of Wellington's position and served as his command during the daytime. In front of the ridge, there were three areas that were pivotal to the war. At the right side, there was a house that was described by the British as a *hollow way*. On the left side, there was an orchard of Hougoumont, a house hidden in the middle of trees. And on the extreme of the left side, there was a hamlet of Papelotte.

Hougoumont and Papelotte served as anchors to the Duke of Wellington's army. Prussians used Papelotte to send reinforcement to the Duke of Wellington's position. The French army, on the other side of the slope, could not see the Duke of Wellington's position, which made the position very secure. On the right area of the French location, there was a village of

Plancenoit, where Napoleon could see the entire battlefield. Simply put, each and every army had their own position that gave them a competitive advantage, which meant the war would be unlike any other.

The Duke of Wellington wrote a letter to Blücher in Brussels, informing him that he would fight with his enemies at Mont-Saint-Jean and could withdraw to Brussels if Blücher failed to give him at least one force. Blücher persuaded some of his soldiers to join the Duke of Wellington's army. With these preparations, the army was ready to fight Napoleon.

Napoleon, on the other hand, was also making his definite plans, the key of which was to strengthen the main army. He decided that the best strategy was to have Grouchy join the main force reserves, and soon he was ready for the war.

Hougoumont

The primary battle began at Hougoumont, the point where the Duke of Wellington and Napoleon clashed. Both armies believed that holding Hougoumont was cardinal to winning the fight, and a war soon ensued.

Napoleon, undoubtedly, had the upper hand, as his mission of ensuring that the Prussians and the British did not meet succeeded. There was a unit that was engaging the Prussians at the opposite side of the battlefield, and Napoleon ensured the Duke of Wellington did not receive any reinforcements.

The European army had experienced more than twenty years of warfare. Therefore, they had well-equipped weapons and skilled swordsmanship. They were, however, inferior to those of France. According to the Duke of Wellington, although they had superior horsemen, they lacked the tactical ability and were inflexible compared to France. Once again, Napoleon had the upper hand.

The French Disintegration

Napoleon was undoubtedly a fearless and confident leader, considering the manner in which he single-handedly fought the Seventh Coalition. At some point, his army had the upper hand, and they may have relaxed, thinking the battle was over. However, the rest of the Duke of Wellington's army, as well as a few Prussians, arrived just when Napoleon was winning, and a fresh and fiercer war erupted. Understandably, this was too much for Napoleon, considering that he was attacked on all sides. As the war continued, it was clear to Napoleon he would not be able to win the war, and the focus shifted from battling to protecting the emperor. As a considerable number fought around Napoleon, the rest concentrated on keeping the aggressors back, and Napoleon lost thousands of fighters in a single day. Some estimates believe that over 33,000 French militants died while the other armies collectively lost half that number.

The Battle of Waterloo marked the beginning of the downfall of Napoleon as the French emperor. So significant was the defeat that multiple sources affirm that he left the battlefield in tears. He abdicated once more, and he was soon taken into exile on the island of Saint Helena.

Exile on Saint Helena

After the abdication of Napoleon following the defeat during the Battle of Waterloo, Napoleon was forced to renounce his throne once again, and he was sent to exile. The banishment marked one of the toughest times Napoleon had ever experienced, especially soon after he realized he would not be exiled in America as he thought, but rather in the midst of the Atlantic. The location was over 1,000 miles from the nearest land, and the coalition did this to ensure he would not have the opportunity to escape once again. The journey to the island took ten weeks, illustrating how far off the island was.

Upon landing, Napoleon was taken to the Longwood House in December 1815, where he wrote and published a paper implying that the British wanted to kill him before his time. Napoleon complained severally in writing that the room was cold, damp, unhealthy, and poor provision to the governor and his custodian. Further, it was infested with very many rats, and Napoleon was sure the British had arranged for the house specifically so they could teach him a lesson.

Napoleon, with his team of followers, dictated his reminiscences and complained about the conditions in Longwood. However, he still had the role of leading the people, as he was given the title of *governor* upon landing. Life in Helen was very different from Elba. At this point, Napoleon did not even want anyone talking about his previous royal position, and he made a decree that no gifts were allowed if they mentioned his imperial status in the least. The people agreed and even made a promise that they would stay with him for as long as he was on the island.

Napoleon stayed for six years on the island until he developed a serious illness. It was later speculated that his illness was brought about by the deplorable conditions that were there, including instances of arsenic poisoning that was in the wallpaper in Longwood House. The arsenic compound that was prevalent in the Longwood wallpaper could probably be what caused the unknown illness, and most people believe that it could have been cancer.

In the course of his time on the island, the French army had made a number of attempts to rescue their emperor, all of which failed. The British knew the distance was not a hindrance to rescue missions, and they took it upon themselves to take control and totally guard the Atlantic. All the plans failed, and Napoleon stayed on the island until his final days.

Death of Napoleon

Napoleon's personal physician stated that the deteriorating health of Napoleon was attributed to poor provision, cold, and dampness that he experienced in Longwood House. However, the main cause of his death was stomach cancer, which could have been genetic and aggravated by the fact that the diet on the island was extremely salty.

Napoleon died on May 18, 1821. The death mask was created around May by an unknown doctor. Napoleon had requested in his will to be buried in the bank of the Seine, and most people wanted his wishes met. However, the British governors stated that Napoleon was to be laid at Saint Helena, in the valley of the willows.

Later, Louis Philippe obtained permission from the British governor to take the remains of the emperor to France. The hearse progressed from the Arc de Triomphe to St. Jerome's Chapel, where his remains were retained until the tomb prepared by Louis Visconti was to be completed. Napoleon's remains were preserved as stone in 1861 at Les Invalides in Paris, where other France military leaders were preserved.

Napoleon's Legacy

It is evident that Napoleon may not have been appreciated enough while he was alive. It was only after his death that most people, his opponents included, realized that a great man had died. So great was his legacy that news confirming his death circulated all over the world. On July 5, *The Times* affirmed that Napoleon was the most extraordinary life known to political history, with military talent that superseded any other that they might have ever seen.

During the same period, the French publication also confirmed that no conqueror had ever had fame extended as much as Napoleon did. His own will had elevated him and ensured his rise among the ranks. The publication also recognized Napoleon as a man who made a solid impression on the minds and the imagination of humankind with an impartial judgment that changed the governance of France forever.

The London examiner portrayed Napoleon as one of the greatest names that ever lived and one whom no one would ever be able to reach in terms of standards and magnificence. The publication went on to hail him as a fearless man who managed to defeat army after army, making him one of the best leaders that ever lived.

While most of Napoleon's legacy is positive, some people still described him as selfish, wanting to subdue all cities and keep France in a constant state of war. While this may be true, it is evident that Napoleon's good deeds superseded the bad, and he is indeed one of the best militants who ever lived.

References

Connelly, O. (2012). The wars of the French Revolution and Napoleon, 1792–1815. Routledge.

de Bourrienne, L. F. (2012). *Memoirs of Napoleon Bonaparte*.

Shanon Selin, S. (2019). How was Napoleon's death reported? Retrieved 12 August 2019, from https://shannonselin.com/2016/05/napoleons-death-reported/

Thompson, J. M. (2018). *Napoleon Bonaparte: His rise and fall*. Pickle Partners Publishing.